FANTASTICALLY faithful HEROES

WHO GAVE THEIR ALL FOR GOD

Paul Kerensa is an award-winning writer of TV, radio, books, and his own stand-up comedy. He is part of the British Comedy Award-winning writing team for the BBC's *Miranda* and the Rose d'Or Award-winning writing team for BBC1's *Not Going Out*. He has written for shows like the BBC's *Top Gear* and Channel 4's *TFI Friday* as well as for BBC Radio 4's *The Now Show* and *Dead Ringers*.

Paul is a regular speaker at Spring Harvest, has toured with the Bible Society, and often does gigs at local churches.

Also in the Fantastically Faithful series:

Fantastically Faithful World Changers
Fantastically Faithful Leaders
Fantastically Faithful Trailblazers

Paul's other books include:

Noah's Car Park Ark
Joe's Bros and the Bus that Goes
Moses and the Exodus Express
Judge Deb and the Battle of the Bands
Planet Protectors! (with Ruth Valerio)
Hark! The Biography of Christmas

PAUL KERENSA

FANTASTICALLY
faithful
HEROES
WHO GAVE THEIR ALL FOR GOD

STARSHINE B★OKS

Text copyright © 2025 Paul Kerensa
Illustrations copyright © 2025 Anglika Dewi Anggreini
This edition copyright © 2025 The Society for Promoting Christian Knowledge

The right of Paul Kerensa to be identified as the author has been asserted by him in accordance with the Copyright, Designs and Patents Act 1988.

All rights reserved. No part of this publication may be reproduced or transmitted in any form or by any means, electronic or mechanical, including photocopy, recording, or any information storage and retrieval system, without permission in writing from the publisher.

Published by **Starshine Books**
Part of the SPCK Group
The Record Hall
16–16A Baldwin's Gardens
London
EC1N 7RJ
www.spck.org.uk

ISBN 978-1-91574-913-0
ebook ISBN 978-1-91574-914-7

Acknowledgements
Scripture quotations are from the ESV Bible (The Holy Bible, English Standard Version), copyright © 2001 by Crossway, a publishing ministry of Good News Publishers. Used by permission. All rights reserved.

Quotations may have been modernised or paraphrased by the author and acknowledgements and copyright notices are provided on p. 104.

First edition 2025

A catalogue record for this book is available from the British Library

Produced on paper from sustainable sources

10 9 8 7 6 5 4 3 2 1

Printed and bound in the UK by Clays Limited
Typeset by Fakenham Prepress Solutions

CONTENTS

Fantastically faithful first thoughts	1
1. Edward Jenner	7
2. Harriet Tubman	18
3. Pandita Ramabai	30
4. John Harper	42
5. Edith Cavell	53
6. Jesse Owens	65
7. Corrie ten Boom	76
8. Martin Luther King, Jr.	88
Fantastically faithful final thoughts	99

FANTASTICALLY FAITHFUL FIRST THOUGHTS

Hello. I'm Paul. I'm just an **ordinary** person. Like all of us, I suppose. Like the people we'll meet in the following pages.

Each one is an ordinary person with an ordinary birth and an ordinary life. At least, to begin with . . .

But then at some point, each of the people in this book did something **EXTRA**ordinary. Well actually, I think they did at least two extraordinary things.

Firstly, each person found FAITH. They puzzled out the world and thought, "Hmm . . . everything makes more sense with God in it." Each one of them put their trust in God and began a lifelong friendship with Jesus.

Secondly, each person faced a **BIG** crisis . . . and then responded to it in an extraordinary way. They left their mark on the world because of WHAT THEY DID NEXT.

Huge events happened in their lives – war, famine, injustice, even shipwrecks – and they had incredible responses, including:

- hiding people in a fake room!
- smuggling speeches on prison toilet paper!
- saving lives by infecting people with a virus!

Sounds crazy, right? But it's all true! Their stories make AMAZING tales. Inspirational ones, too.

So who are we talking about? And what does the title of this book mean? Let's answer both questions at the same time. Here are our fantastically faithful HEROES who gave their all for God:

FANTASTICALLY – Each one of them was "fantastic" . . . and each one was an "ally"! That means they were a supportive friend to those around them (especially those who were struggling) . . .

. . . like Jesse Owens, the world's greatest athlete, who smashed records and stood up to the ugliest power on the planet and inspired his competitors.

But "fantastic" doesn't mean "fantasy". These are real stories and real lives. Sometimes the people might sound SUPERHUMAN, but they're just human, like you and me. We might not all run as fast as Jesse, but we can have his determination and strength to do what's right. And what is right? Well, maybe we should ask God. Which means being . . .

FAITHFUL – Each person in this book is FULL of faith. Some of them grew up going to church. One or two even had parents who were ministers. We'll meet some whose faith changed as they studied religion, while others may have never read a word of the Bible, but heard it read aloud instead . . .

. . . **like Harriet Tubman:** so full of FAITH that, as she ran away from her enslavers, she called out in prayer asking God which way to run! You may have prayed before, but probably not like that.

The people in this book didn't necessarily know God any better than you or I do, but they trusted that he would show them the way (literally, in Harriet's case. Turn left here!).

HEROES – Forget superheroes. You don't need to fly, spin webs, or turn green to be brave enough to improve people's lives. We'll meet REAL heroes . . .

. . . **like Edith Cavell**, the wartime nurse who helped patients in hospital, then helped them out of hospital and into safe countries. "Not all heroes wear capes," people say. Well, Edith did – a nurse's cape! (Nurses wore capes back then. Some of the time. Let's assume she wore a cape. It makes the hero thing work well.)

WHO – Who were these people? Some you may have heard of, but others led quieter lives . . .

. . . **like John Harper**, a Scottish church minister who probably wouldn't be remembered except for the fact that he boarded a very famous ship: RMS *Titanic*.

We'll get behind the stories to find out the WHO behind the WHAT: who these historical figures were, where they came from, where they were going, and who they met and influenced along the way.

GAVE – Generosity is at the heart of each of our stories. Each of these heroes was so giving . . .

    . . . **like Martin Luther King, Jr.**, a church minister who gave time and energy not just to his church community, but to the wider community, too – then the city, the state, the country, and eventually the world. He gave great thought and attention to the huge injustices of the day. He gave his all in every campaign he led. And he gave his life for what he believed in.

THEIR – Each person used THEIR gifts and THEIR skills to benefit others . . .

    . . . **like Edward Jenner,** the doctor who used his talents to save millions of lives. He knew what he could do best, and he turned that into a gift for humanity. He also knew that his medical skills had been given to him by God so, after his breakthrough, he gave away his great creation.

All of our heroes in this book had unique skills – truly THEIRS. (Pssst! Guess what? You have unique skills, too . . .)

ALL – These heroes didn't just use one bit of their lives to change other people's lives for the better. They didn't just do what they did on Monday lunchtimes or whenever they felt like it. They did it all the time. And they gave all of themselves – their personalities, abilities, and identities . . .

. . . **like Pandita Ramabai**, the scholar and activist (someone who does a lot of political or social campaigning) who used her unique experiences to improve the lives of others on several continents. Wherever she went, she truly brought all of herself, including her cultural background (and her daughter, too!). So whenever she spoke or campaigned, you got all of her.

FOR – Their achievements weren't for themselves. They acted FOR others . . .

. . . **like Corrie ten Boom**, the watchmaker who helped anyone who came to her door in desperation. She didn't think twice about risking her own life FOR others. She followed the example of Jesus, living a life of self-sacrifice. She didn't do anything to be famous or to look good; she just worked FOR those around her. Living FOR others might be the opposite of what the world's culture promotes today. Forget selfies and "living my best life". How about living for someone else's best life? Oh, and who were all our heroes working for, above everything . . . ?

GOD – Our creator, sustainer, champion, and friend. The real HERO of this book!

There's another hero in this story: you.

You can be just like the people in these pages. None of them started out thinking they'd be HEROES, and yet they were.

I hope you enjoy reading about their amazing lives as much as I did, and that you will be inspired by their stories to be brave in small things, and even in the **NOT-SO-SMALL** things.

To help with this, at the end of each chapter, there are a few questions for you to think about, a short Bible passage to read, and a prayer to bring everything together before God.

Because we all start off ordinary. The **EXTRA**ordinariness comes in because of what we DO, how we RESPOND to situations, and how we TREAT others around us.

Want proof? Let's meet the team . . .

CHAPTER 1

EDWARD JENNER

(1749-1823)

Can you imagine what it feels like to **save** a life? How about saving a hundred lives, or hundreds? That must be amazing. What if you saved **MILLIONS** of lives?

This is the story of Edward Jenner: a **GENEROUS** English doctor who made an amazing discovery. It's said that Edward saved more lives than anyone else in history.

It's also a story about a boy named James, a milkmaid named Sarah, and a cow named Blossom. It's **gross**, it's **AMAZING**, and it's an **EPIC** tale of living out faith in God.

Edward was born in 1749 into a church family. His father was the local vicar and young Edward grew up with a great **FAITH** in God. He wanted to help others, but he also needed to earn money, so he trained to become a doctor.

Now we meet the villain of the story: smallpox. For something **small**, it was **MIGHTY**. It had been around for thousands of years – even Egyptian mummies had it – and had taken millions of lives.

Everyone knew about the **DANGERS** of smallpox. About a third of people who caught it died from it. Another third lost their sight, and many of the "lucky" survivors ended up with very nasty scars all over their skin.

There was no cure, so people just hoped that if they caught it, it would be a mild version. In fact, anyone who did catch a mild version became very *popular*! People would visit them in the hope of also catching just a minor case. Yes, a case of even-smaller-pox (no one called it that).

Do you want to know what people did to deliberately catch that disease? Do you REALLY want to know? It's a bit disgusting . . .

(**WARNING**: Skip this paragraph if you don't like *disgusting* things.)

Someone would take an infected person's scab, squeeze pus out of it, then smear it onto their own skin. Horrid! (Oh, and don't try this at home.) But it worked, a bit, some of the time. Some people lived, some died, some caught a milder version of smallpox.

(**ATTENTION**: Read from here again; there are no more disgusting bits. Well, not many. Alright, there's one bit in a minute . . .)

For those who survived smallpox – good NEWS! Catch it once, and you won't catch it again. For years this was the only way to battle it. As a child, Edward was deliberately infected with smallpox, but as he grew up he thought of a better idea.

Edward was endlessly CURIOUS, and he loved nature. He was even asked to join Captain James Cook's famous exploration to Australia as part of his scientific team. Edward turned him down, preferring to stay in England's countryside. Here he became fascinated with birds, especially the cuckoo. (Well, cuckoos are incredible. How do they fit inside those CLOCKS and how do they tell the time? What a bird!)

He noticed something else unusual about the natural world around him, too, to do with local farm workers and, in particular, a milkmaid called Sarah Nelmes.

The story goes that, like many milkmaids, Sarah had unusually clear skin, which was unusual because so many people had scars and scabs thanks to diseases like smallpox. Why was Sarah's skin so smooth? Did milkmaids rub milk into their faces? No. Did farmers only hire smooth-skinned milkmaids? Again, no. Were milkmaids just so glad to be working in the great outdoors that it showed in their beautiful skin? No, no, NO.

Sarah herself gave Edward the reason: "I shall never have smallpox, for I have had cowpox." She had caught this mild disease from one of her cows, called Blossom.

So what was cowpox? It made people unwell, but it wasn't as bad as smallpox. As the name suggests, it came from cows (though chickenpox does not come from chickens!). In this case, cowpox had come from Blossom the cow and gone to Sarah the milkmaid. It was common knowledge in the milkmaid community that cowpox had a great upside: if you caught it, you wouldn't catch smallpox.

Edward wanted to know MORE. In 1796, he wondered if a tiny dose of cowpox might prevent people from catching the more serious smallpox. To find out, he did an experiment. One that we would **NOT** do today!

Edward's gardener's son was eight-year-old James Phipps . . . and he was about to make HISTORY in the most disgusting way. Edward took pus from Sarah's cowpox-infected hand and infected James with it. (That's the other *disgusting* bit! All in the name of science.)

James felt a bit ill but quickly recovered, as people did with COWPOX. But Edward wasn't finished with James yet. Six weeks later, he deliberately gave James SMALLPOX. Incredibly, James didn't fall ill at all. Because he'd already had cowpox, the smallpox did **nothing**.

Poor James had to go through being given smallpox again and again – **TWENTY** more times – as Edward wanted absolute proof that, having had cowpox, he wouldn't get ill with smallpox. He didn't!

Edward told other doctors and scientists of his new discovery. Naming it after the Latin word for cow –

vacca – Edward called this new breakthrough a "VACCINE". Vaccinations, then, are named after cows, and not just any old

cows, but Blossom the cow – perhaps the most important cow who EVER lived!

The experts took some convincing. A lot of people thought Edward was crazy. Cruel cartoons were drawn to mock him. They showed people who dared to try his new discovery with cows' heads growing out of them! Edward said: "I am not surprised that men are not thankful to me; but I wonder that they are not GRATEFUL to God for the good which he has made me the instrument of conveying to my fellow-creatures."

OTHER PIONEERS

There were others who had experimented with preventing smallpox before Edward. Farmer Benjamin Jesty and Doctor John Fewster both deliberately infected people with cowpox to stop smallpox. Surgeon Daniel Sutton set up some clinics, too. But none of them persevered with their work or shouted about it like Edward did. And none of them had a cow called Blossom.

Edward's idea was new, and people were unsure, but eventually his new vaccination idea spread throughout Britain and Europe and across the WORLD. Millions of lives were saved.

But here's the AMAZING part. (As if the rest wasn't already amazing!) Because of Edward's great FAITH in God, he gave away his discovery, refusing to make any money from it. He could have been rich! But he preferred to serve God and help other people, even if it meant he often had no money himself. He set up a free vaccination clinic in his back garden, in a small summerhouse he called the Temple of Vaccinia. This was the world's first vaccination clinic. You can still visit it today! (They no longer give out vaccines there . . . but they do have a nice gift shop.)

Edward's vaccine journeyed around the world. Outbreaks of smallpox were **stopped** by spreading the cowpox vaccine. Sometimes cowpox-infected children were sent into villages to help spread the mild illness, which then stopped the more serious one.

People didn't think Edward was *crazy* any more. The president of the USA, Thomas Jefferson, thanked him. The French leader, Napoleon, was so grateful for the

SMALLPOX TODAY . . .

There is no smallpox today. It took nearly 200 years, but the last case was in 1977. In 1980, the World Health Organization announced that smallpox was no more! It's still the only human disease that we've completely wiped off the face of the planet.

vaccine that he freed British soldiers he had captured. If Edward wouldn't take payment, he could have some free prisoners instead!

In his later years, Edward became the king's doctor and went back to studying birds. He was FAMOUS the world over and became known as "the Grandfather of Vaccinations".

Edward's Christian faith was there throughout EVERYTHING he did. Every decision he made – from deciding to become a doctor, to trying to save people from smallpox, to giving away his vaccines for free – was driven by the thought: what would God want me to do? Above all, he didn't work for fame or celebrity status. He worked for the glory of God. And he saved MILLIONS.

"I AM A FOLLOWER
OF CHRIST.
I AM A TOOL IN THE
HANDS OF GOD."

EDWARD JENNER

THINK

- If you could create or invent something to make the world a better place, what would it be? Where would you start?
- How do you think God wants us to behave with our money and possessions?

READ

Each one must give as he has decided in his heart, not reluctantly or under compulsion, for God loves a cheerful giver.

2 Corinthians 9:7

PRAY

Healing God,

Thank you for the kind help of James, Sarah, and Blossom the cow in discovering a cure for smallpox. Thank you for the genius and generosity of Edward Jenner. Above all, thank you for your overflowing generosity in giving us your son, Jesus. Help us to help each other, and to be generous to all, just as Edward was.

Amen.

CHAPTER 2

HARRIET TUBMAN

(ABOUT 1822–1913)

How **brave** would you have to be to escape from slavery, then help others to escape too? How about doing this **13 TIMES**?

This is the story of Harriet Tubman, a **COURAGEOUS** African American woman who was born into slavery but was determined to be free. Harriet took great risks to find a better future – not only for herself, but for countless others, too.

It's also a story about a lead weight, two chickens, and an invisible train. Can you see it? No, me *neither*. But it was there. Oh boy, was it there!

When Harriet was born she was given the name Araminta, but she later became known as Harriet, so we'll call her that. She was born around 1822 but we don't know the **exact** year, as there was no official record of her birth. This was because her parents – her mother, Rit (short for Harriet), and her father, Ben – were both enslaved. So Harriet also became a victim of slavery, from the very **moment** she was born.

Harriet didn't go to school. Instead she went to work. **HARD** work. When she was five, her job was to rock the enslavers' baby to sleep each night, and to keep rocking that cradle through the night. If the baby woke and **cried**, Harriet was whipped.

Sometimes Harriet worked outside, doing **HEAVY** labour in the fields. It was a horrid, painful existence. It was even more painful when she went shopping one day . . .

Harriet was buying some groceries with the overseer – the man in charge of her – when they saw a man **ESCAPING** from slavery. Harriet wanted the man to get away, and even tried to help, but the overseer threw a huge two-pound weight (about 1kg) to try and stop him. It hit Harriet right on the head, giving her a headache that lasted her whole life. But it also gave her a new **VISION** of a possible future – one of **FREEDOM**.

Harriet began to **hear** the voice of God. She had never been taught to read, so she couldn't read the Bible, but her mother had always told her

Bible stories. The one she loved most was the tale of Moses and the Exodus – it was a wonderful story that filled her with HOPE.

In 1849, Harriet decided it was time to ESCAPE her life of slavery. The man who enslaved her had just died, and like the other people he claimed to "own", she was to be "sold" and perhaps sent far away from her family. First, she escaped with her brothers, but they decided to return to their families, so Harriet had to return with them. The next time, she decided to go by herself. She hinted to others of her plans during her last day of work, saying, "I'll meet you in the morning. I'm bound for the Promised Land."

For Harriet, the PROMISED LAND she was headed for was Pennsylvania, going via the Underground Railroad. And this was where the invisible train came in . . .

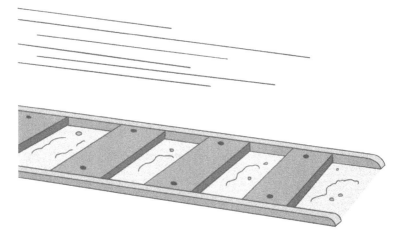

MOSES AND THE EXODUS

Thousands of years ago, Moses grew up seeing his Israelite friends and family enslaved and treated horrifically by the Egyptians. He attacked a slave driver, then ran away.

God spoke to Moses through a burning bush, and sent him back to his people. He was to tell the Egyptian pharaoh to free the enslaved Israelites. When the pharaoh refused, ten plagues fell upon Egypt, including flies, locusts, a blood-red river, and even the death of Pharaoh's son.

That was enough to convince Pharaoh, so the Israelites were free to go . . . at first. But Pharaoh changed his mind and his troops chased after the Israelites. God told Moses to raise his staff for the Red Sea to part, and the Israelites walked safely through. They were free! A new Promised Land awaited them . . .

You can read the full story in the book of Exodus in the Bible.

This was not a *real* railroad, and there were no actual trains – alright, not even *invisible* ones . . .

Harriet travelled by night, following the North Star. The journey was nearly 90 miles and took **MANY** days.

THE UNDERGROUND RAILROAD

This was the nickname for a trail across the USA in the 1800s. It wasn't a railroad, and it wasn't even underground! But it was a big secret.

Some states had slavery and others didn't, so enslaved people tried to escape to "free states" – states where slavery had been abolished. At the time, they were called "runaways", but we might better think of them as freedom seekers.

Freedom seekers (or "passengers") would follow known routes, stopping at safe houses where those on their side ("conductors") would house them, hide them, and direct them on.

It was very dangerous. It took many weeks, many miles, and a lot of risk-taking to make the long journey to a safer land.

Do you think this sounds like the "Promised Land" from the Moses story? Harriet spotted that, too.

Eventually, she reached Pennsylvania. She couldn't believe the new-found FREEDOM she felt as soon as she crossed into the new state, saying: "There was such a **GLORY**

over everything; the sun came like gold through the trees, and over the fields, and I felt like I was in HEAVEN."

But she instantly felt very alone. "I ain't got no friend but you!" she shouted to God in prayer. "Come to my HELP, Lord!"

God did come to Harriet's aid – countless times – because the path ahead wasn't to be found in this world of newfound freedom. In fact, for Harriet the road ahead was the road BEHIND her, back the way she'd come.

Harriet did a very **BOLD** thing indeed. After she'd earned money doing local jobs, she turned around and returned to Maryland. Her own freedom was not enough. She thought of her friends and family, still enslaved. So, she snuck back.

First, Harriet helped her niece and her niece's children escape, then on a second trip she helped one of her brothers, Moses. But very soon she was the one to take the nickname "Moses".

Over the next **TEN YEARS**, Harriet helped her brothers, sisters-in-law, nieces, nephews, and parents, plus MANY others who wanted to escape north. She journeyed in winter, at night, so the roads were quieter. She used disguises – often dressed as an old woman or carrying two live chickens, as if she were on the way to market.

On one occasion, Harriet was walking near the place where she was once enslaved when she recognized an enslaver walking towards her. She could **NOT** let him lock eyes with her. So what did she do? She made the chickens squawk! In all the chaos, nobody was looking at her, and the enslaver was distracted by the two squawking birds. PHEW! This was just one of her many highly dangerous escapades . . . but it only became more dangerous.

A law was passed stating that, even in free states, anyone HELPING those seeking freedom could be arrested. The whole of the USA suddenly became riskier for people like Harriet. Did she stop? NO! She just went further north, taking her rescued friends and family to Canada. Each person who crossed the border into freedom did so to the

sound of Harriet crying out: "GLORY to God, and Jesus too! One more soul is safe!"

Throughout, Harriet prayed and TRUSTED God for protection. Sometimes, when she was trying to run away from her pursuers, she even shouted aloud to ask God for directions! Whatever God told her, it clearly worked. Harriet rescued about 70 enslaved people and helped with the escape of about 70 more.

In the 1860s, the American Civil War raged. It was American, and it was a war – but it was **not** very civil! There was nothing polite about this war. It was "civil" because it was between citizens living in the same country – in this case between people who supported slavery and those who wanted to abolish it.

Harriet served in the Union army (unsurprisingly, this was the side that wanted to abolish slavery), becoming the FIRST African American woman to do so. She began as a cook and a nurse, but soon became a **spy** and a scout. Her knowledge of the Underground Railroad's secret trails proved incredibly useful. After all, she'd already pretty much been a spy for more than a decade.

Sometimes her information led to army raids on property where people were enslaved, so the more operations she helped with, the more people were FREED. She even led some military expeditions, becoming the **FIRST** woman to do so. Once called Araminta, then Harriet, then Moses, she now had a new nickname: "General Tubman".

When she was an actual old woman (rather than disguised as one!), Harriet campaigned for women's rights and the rights of African Americans, and set up a home for those who had been enslaved.

Throughout her dramatic life of twists and turns, Harriet always TRUSTED God to show her the way – sometimes literally. Who needs an app to tell you to turn left or right when God can instead? It's all part of her COURAGEOUS life of faith that helped countless people, and throughout she never stopped praying.

"IT WASN'T ME, IT WAS THE LORD! I ALWAYS TOLD HIM, 'I TRUST TO YOU. I DON'T KNOW WHERE TO GO OR WHAT TO DO, BUT I EXPECT YOU TO LEAD ME.' AND HE ALWAYS DID."

HARRIET TUBMAN

THINK

- Harriet was inspired by the story of Moses. Which Bible character are you inspired by? If you could be nicknamed after anyone from the Bible, who would it be?
- How did Harriet speak to God? Try speaking to God throughout your day. You don't need special words! You can just speak to him the way you would speak to a close friend.

READ

Whatever you ask in prayer, you will receive, if you have faith.

Matthew 21:22

PRAY

Saving God, who brought the Israelites into the Promised Land, and who sets the captives free,

Thank you for the life and service of Harriet Tubman. Thank you that we can speak to you when we need direction and help. Help us to help others, and to put our faith in you, just as Harriet did.

Amen.

CHAPTER 3

PANDITA RAMABAI
(1858-1922)

Imagine being told that because you're a woman, you're not good enough. That because your husband has died, your life is pretty much over. Imagine converting from one religion to another, but not feeling you belong in either. Imagine being an outsider, but instead of just changing yourself, changing the SYSTEM! Now imagine doing all this in the 1800s on three continents and in several languages . . . as a single mother.

This is the story of Pandita Ramabai, a DEDICATED Indian woman who was a scholar, a social reformer, a widow, a mother, and a HERO. Society didn't treat her well, so she turned her experience into a chance to make other people's lives better.

It's also a story about a baby, a pile of books, and a beautiful Indian sari. Intelligent and INSPIRATIONAL, Pandita was in a league of her own . . . and not just in terms of fashion!

Pandita Ramabai was born in 1858 in south-west India. In fact, when she was born, she was given the name Rama, then the "bai" was added as a term of respect to make "Ramabai", and then she was given the name Pandita – you'll find out why later. We'll call her Pandita from the start.

Reading the holy books was very important in Pandita's priestly Hindu family, but traditionally this was ONLY done by men. Yet her father was keen for girls to be EDUCATED, so he taught Pandita Sanskrit, the sacred language of Hinduism.

Then the family took her SKILLS on tour! They weren't exactly putting on shows, but it became a sort of performance, as Pandita and her brother recited from the ancient Sanskrit holy books, impressing crowds with their knowledge.

Pandita's family were members of the Brahmin caste, which meant they were highly respected and people listened to them.

When Pandita was 16 there was a GREAT famine, and both her mother and father died, so Pandita and her brother continued to travel and make money by performing their Sanskrit "show". Then her brother died, too. Soon after, she married a lawyer. After such unhappy times, you might think people would have been HAPPY for her, but her husband

THE CASTE SYSTEM

In Indian Hindu culture, the ancient caste system divided society into four (well, five – see below) groups. It decided who you could marry and work with, and generally planned your life out for you.

At the top of the system were Brahmins: priests, scholars, and judges who studied the Hindu holy books. Next came Kshatriya: warriors, military leaders, or rulers. Then Vaishyas: traders, farmers, and others with skilled jobs. At the bottom were Shudras: the workers.

Below the bottom were Dalits, who didn't even qualify as one of the four official castes, and were sometimes called "untouchables". They did the worst jobs, like scrubbing toilets and skinning dead animals.

The caste system kept everyone in their place, whether they liked it or not. And even though she was a Brahmin at the top of the tree, Pandita didn't like it at all . . .

was from a lower caste, so society at large looked **down** on her. She was **ignored** and **shunned**. But worse was to come . . .

After just a year of marriage, Pandita's husband died, too. This was not only *very* sad for her, but also meant she was expected to shave her head, wear only white to show she was a widow, and fade into the background. Now she was **REALLY** ignored and **REALLY** shunned. "Pandita? Pandita who? Never heard of her . . . "

At only 23 years old, Pandita had lost so much – from her family to her place in society. But she had gained a few things, too. First, she now had a GREAT REPUTATION for her knowledge of the Hindu scriptures and for public speaking. It was for this reason that she was given the name "Pandita", meaning "scholar". Second, her marriage had given her a baby daughter called Manorama.

Pandita was now a single mother, with no family except Manorama. Perhaps that's why she felt she could go anywhere and do anything, despite society saying she should be doing less, not more. She was in demand as a speaker and a teacher, and set up an organization promoting education for women.

Many girls were married between the ages of ten and twelve! Pandita thought that was **SHOCKINGLY** young and suggested that education would give girls a better future.

She knew this would not be popular. "In 99 cases out of 100," she said, "the educated men of this country are opposed to female education and the proper position of women."

At a time when women and girls were expected to be seen and not heard, Pandita wanted to be heard in several languages . . . in fact, she learned SEVEN!

In the early 1880s, Pandita published her first book, and her speeches and writings even reached QUEEN VICTORIA in the UK, 4,000 miles away.

Pandita also thought it was HUGELY unfair that Indian women couldn't train to be doctors, especially because in hospitals women could only be treated by women! Hoping to train as a doctor herself, she went to England with Manorama. She was turned down for medical training, though – either because of her race, her gender, or her disability (she was slowly losing her hearing). Whatever the reason, she felt the unfairness deeply, which spurred her on even more.

In England she was baptized, having given her life to Jesus and become a Christian. The Hindu holy books she read as a child had asked questions about life, the universe, and EVERYTHING, but she felt they didn't answer the questions as well as Christianity did. Christianity made sense to her and offered what she thought was a fairer role for women. She also saw that the Christian community she stayed with cared IMPRESSIVELY for poor women, so Pandita wanted in.

But she didn't immediately fit in. The nuns she spent time with had MORE "dos and don'ts" for her – not the same as the "dos and don'ts" of the Hindu religion of her youth – and she was asked to change what she ate and wore.

Pandita **RESISTED**, and clung to the vegetarian diet of her upbringing. She wanted to wear a crucifix with a Sanskrit inscription, but was given one with Latin words. And she refused to change what she wore: a **BEAUTIFUL** sari.

While wearing this dress, she set sail for America for the graduation of the *first* female Indian doctor, a relative of hers. If women couldn't graduate as doctors in the UK, they at least could in America!

Pandita and Manorama stayed in America so Pandita was able to speak and write about how life could be **BETTER** for women across the *world* – especially back in India – and she wrote another book, called *The High-Caste Hindu Woman*. It was in America that she met someone you may remember . . . Harriet Tubman! Yes, Pandita and Harriet became friends – both eager to help poor women escape the situations they were trapped in so they could have a **BRIGHTER** future.

With her daughter ever by her side, Pandita returned to India in 1889. She was now an **INTERNATIONALLY RECOGNIZED** social reformer, with enough money to open a home and a school where young widows could be given a good education.

Another famine struck in the 1890s, so Pandita again reached out to those who needed help. She rescued orphans, young widows (who of course could still be children themselves!), homeless or displaced people, those with disabilities such as blindness, and **ANYONE** else she felt society had forgotten. By 1900, there were **1,500** people being cared for at her shelter, which she had called Mukti, meaning "freedom" or "salvation".

Pandita kept reading and
writing books, and she kept
studying the Bible. One of her
last projects was to translate
the Bible into her local
language, Marathi.

Throughout her life,
Pandita was **TRULY
HERSELF** – dressing and
eating the way she wanted, rooted in
her past. But she gave her life over to become the woman
she felt God wanted her to be, helping people neglected
by society. From her early and later years in India, to her
time and conversion in the UK, to her work in the USA, she
gave countless people a brighter future. The Pandita
Ramabai Mukti Mission is still going STRONG today,
continuing Pandita's work by caring for those in need
of help.

"A LIFE TOTALLY COMMITTED TO GOD HAS NOTHING TO FEAR, NOTHING TO LOSE, NOTHING TO REGRET."

PANDITA RAMABAI

THINK

- Pandita sometimes felt as if she didn't fit in. When is it OK not to fit in? How should we treat other people who don't fit in?
- Pandita's faith inspired her to help people in need. What could you do to help people in need in your community?

READ

Learn to do good;
seek justice,
correct oppression;
bring justice to the fatherless,
plead the widow's cause.

> Isaiah 1:17

PRAY

Loving God,

You hold all people in need in your heart. Thank you for the life of Pandita Ramabai and for her work to give many thousands of people a hopeful future. Bless the work of the Pandita Ramabai Mukti Mission today. Help us to care for people in need, especially those in need of education, equality, security, and hope.

    Amen.

CHAPTER 4

JOHN HARPER

(1872–1912)

What do you do in an **emergency**? Do you panic? Run away? Look after yourself? It's normal to want to protect ourselves in a crisis, but how can we help **OTHERS**, with calm and care, just when they need it? Perhaps our next HERO will show us . . .

This is the story of John Harper, a FAITHFUL Scottish pastor who unfortunately boarded a very famous ship, RMS *Titanic*. But fortunately for others, John was able to help and comfort those around him in their darkest moments.

It's also a story about a ticket, a lifeboat, and a life jacket. But at his end, John had nothing; nothing, that is except for a **HUGE** love for God, which he shared with everyone around him!

John Harper was born in 1872 in Houston – not the big city in the USA, but a small village in Renfrewshire, Scotland.

John had a Christian upbringing, and as a teenager he decided for himself that he believed in God and wanted to tell **EVERYONE** about him. So, aged 18, he became a preacher.

By 25, he was leading a church in Glasgow that started with 25 people but soon grew to 20 TIMES that size! John married a dressmaker called Annie and they had a daughter, also named Annie but known, confusingly, as Nana. She was not John's nana . . . she was his daughter!

Annie died when Nana was just a few days old, so John brought Nana up on his **own**. Father and daughter journeyed together as he preached, along with Nana's grown-up cousin Jessie, who helped look after her.

One day John received an invitation. Would he travel across the Atlantic to preach in Chicago? John said that if Nana and Jessie could come too, then **YES!**

Growing up, John had experienced a few incidents with water. Aged two, he had fallen into a well, but was rescued by his mother. In his 20s, he was carried out to sea by a strong current, then back to shore again. In his 30s, his ship sprang a leak in the Mediterranean Sea. You might think this

43

would have put him off the water, but now he was about to head across the Atlantic . . . on RMS *Titanic*.

As John, Nana (now aged six), and Jessie waited to board the **HUGE** ship at Southampton dock, they had no idea what lay ahead.

We can imagine that John had an *enjoyable* first few days at sea. Some nice food, a walk on deck, and the occasional selfie (alright, maybe this was a bit early for selfies).

He certainly attended the Sunday morning church service and, as always, urged others to put their FAITH in Jesus.

On its fourth night at sea, *Titanic* hit a MASSIVE iceberg. It should have been easy to miss – it was many times bigger than *Titanic* – but the ship was going too fast to turn.

When the ALARM sounded, John ran to the bedroom to wake Jessie and Nana. Soon they were putting on life jackets and rushing to the deck. John helped them up a ladder and into a lifeboat, but he stayed on *Titanic*.

As panic steadily spread across the doomed ship, John SHOUTED for women, children, and those who didn't know Jesus to board the lifeboats. He made sure those who were **not ready** to meet their maker were the first to escape.

But *Titanic* didn't have enough lifeboats – and too many left early, half-empty. The world's greatest ship, thought to be unsinkable and on its very first voyage, was not equipped for such a DISASTER.

When *Titanic* began to sink, there was no **way to** save those left on board. But while others panicked and tried to save themselves, John was a voice of CALM.

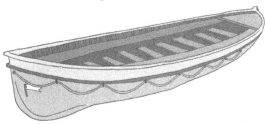

45

"THE UNSINKABLE"

RMS *Titanic* was the world's largest passenger steam ship and launched to great fanfare in April 1912. RMS stands for "Royal Mail Ship" because as well as carrying people, it also carried mail.

The ship was spacious and luxurious. In first class there was a gym, a Turkish bath, a barber shop, and the first ever onboard swimming pool. Second-class passengers could enjoy afternoon tea in the library, walk along the outdoor promenade, and listen to a pianist as they ate their meals. Even the third-class passengers were provided with food – on most ships they had to bring their own – and a piano, but no one played for them. They had to make their own music.

There were, however, only 20 lifeboats on board, which could hold 1,178 people. Yet when *Titanic* set sail there were 2,240 people on board . . .

He kept preaching the gospel, saying the same phrase from the Bible to anyone he met: "BELIEVE in the Lord Jesus, and you will be SAVED!" (Acts 16:31).

He repeated these words to passenger after passenger on the sloping deck. As they fled for their lives, he wanted them to know God and to know the COMFORT of heaven.

Soon the ship broke in half and hurtled underwater. Any remaining passengers went down with it, jumped, or were flung into the water.

John had **no** life jacket – he had given his to another man, wanting him to live ... and BELIEVE. Even as he swam in the icy Atlantic waters, clutching bits of wreckage from the ship as a float, he continued telling people the GOOD NEWS of Jesus, just as he had on board. He saw a fellow passenger trying to survive, clinging to a wooden pole that had once been part of a sail.

"Man!" he cried to him. "Are you SAVED?"

"No, I am not!" said the man in the pitch black of night.

"Believe in the Lord Jesus, and you will be saved!" John HOLLERED, as a wave threw him away, out of sight. But a few minutes later, the waves swept the two men up against each other again.

"Are you saved NOW?" John called again to the man.

"No," came the shivering reply.

AND THE BAND PLAYED ON . . .

John Harper wasn't the only one to stay on the ship, continuing his duties – in his case, saving souls. Others had work to do, too:

Captain Smith went down with the ship, after releasing his crew from their duties.

Jack Phillips and Harold Bride, the ship's radio operators, kept sending distress signals to nearby ships. They sent one of the first new "SOS" messages.

Wallace Hartley led the band that famously kept playing to calm the passengers. It's thought their last song may have been the hymn "Nearer, My God, to Thee".

Hundreds more crew members deliberately stayed off the lifeboats so the passengers could flee.

"Believe in the Lord Jesus, and you will be saved," repeated John – his last words before **slipping** underwater from the wreckage.

There and then, that man clinging to the pole PRAYED for the first time. A few minutes later, with the water **calmer**, a lifeboat returned, and the man was pulled out of the water. Later, at a reunion of *Titanic* survivors, he told his story: "I TRUSTED Christ. I am John Harper's last convert."

Jessie and Nana survived, too. Their lifeboat was picked up by another ship, which eventually rescued 706 of the people on board *Titanic*.

John's belief in God supported him through life's stormy seas. His faith was OVERFLOWING and he couldn't wait to SHARE it with others, even in his last moments.

As for his niece Jessie, she thought back to John's last night on the ship. As he had looked out at the setting sun **dipping** below the horizon, he had true and certain FAITH that the next day would be nothing but beautiful.

"IT WILL BE BEAUTIFUL
IN THE MORNING."

JOHN HARPER

THINK

- John Harper kept repeating "Believe in the Lord Jesus, and you will be saved" (Acts 16:31). It was his most-loved Bible verse. Do you have a Bible verse you love best?
- John loved Jesus so much that he wanted everyone he met to love Jesus, too! How could you share Jesus' love with your friends?

READ

And Jesus said to them, "Go into all the world and proclaim the gospel to the whole creation."

Mark 16:15

PRAY

Loving God,

Thank you for loving us so much that you gave us your son, Jesus. Thank you for the dedication and faith of John Harper, who shared your love with people in their time of need. Help us to bring your message of hope and joy to people we know and love, and to new people.

Amen.

CHAPTER 5

EDITH CAVELL

(1865-1915)

Do you treat everyone equally? People on your side AND people against you? What if you knew that your life would be at risk if you did so? Would you stop, or would you help even more people? During the First World War, there was a nurse who did just that, in the toughest of conditions.

This is the story of Edith Cavell, a DEVOTED English nurse with a passion for helping people – helping EVERYONE, whoever they were! She paid the HIGHEST price for it because she knew it was the right thing to do.

It's also a story about a medal and a hospital, and tragically it ends with a blindfold. But a lot of lives were saved in between.

Edith Cavell was born in 1865 in the small village of Swardeston, not far from England's east coast. Her father was the local vicar, so she grew up going to church a lot! She had a HAPPY childhood with her younger brother and sisters, and a good education, showing a TALENT for art and French.

In her 20s she worked as a governess in Brussels, Belgium, teaching children from a wealthy family. This also gave her the opportunity to speak LOTS of French, which is widely spoken in Belgium.

But a visit home in 1895 was life-changing. Have you ever tried something and just known it was the right thing for you? Well, Edith did, and for her it was nursing her ill father. It wasn't exactly a great hobby, but she discovered she was GREAT at it and that she loved helping people. So when her father recovered, Edith decided to train as a nurse.

While she was training, there was an outbreak of a DEADLY disease called typhoid in the town of Maidstone. Edith and other nurses rushed to help. The high standard of nursing that the patients received from Edith SAVED many people from dying. This earned Edith and the other nurses a "Maidstone Medal". It was also good training for nursing in a CRISIS.

After ten years of nursing, Edith became a matron (a nurse who was in charge of the other nurses). The role of matron also gave her CRUCIAL skills in leadership and organization. She later went on not only to help save lives, but to help **OTHER** nurses save lives too.

In 1907, Edith returned to Belgium to become a matron at a new nursing school. **Professional** nursing was new to Belgium. Until then, healthcare had often been provided by nuns or other religious groups. Edith **TAUGHT** nurses in three hospitals and took nursing in Belgium into the modern era. She was known for being rather **strict** with her students, but they **RESPECTED** her and her belief that you should think less of yourself and more of others.

There was a new **disaster** coming that would need a **LOT** of nurses and a **LOT** of help. No one knew it yet, but the First World War was on its way.

On 4 August 1914, when war was announced, Edith was home in Norfolk visiting her mother. She could have stayed there, but she knew where she was **MOST** needed: back at her hospital in Belgium, a country now **occupied** by Germany.

Edith arrived to find that her workplace had been **converted** into a Red Cross hospital, helping soldiers injured

THE WORLD GOES TO WAR

In 1914, the world went to war.

In June, Archduke Franz Ferdinand, heir to the Austro–Hungarian throne, was shot by a Serbian man. So, the Austro–Hungarian army went to war with Serbia.

Russia was allied with Serbia, and Germany was allied with the Austro–Hungarian empire, so they entered the war too, fighting against each other.

France was allied with Russia, so that put Germany against France. In August, Germany invaded Belgium to get to France.

Britain was allied with France and Belgium, so Britain declared war on Germany.

That all happened quickly. What a summer! More than 30 nations became involved in what we now know as the First World War (sadly, there was a Second World War not long after). It lasted four years, and more than 16 million people died.

in the war, as well as civilians. Whether British, French, Belgian, or German, Edith helped EVERYoNE IN NEED, no matter which side they were fighting for. She told the other nurses, "ANY wounded soldier must be treated, friend or foe. Each man is a father, husband or son. As nurses you must take no part in the quarrel – our work is for HUMANITY."

Within weeks she heard of two wounded BRITISH soldiers who were in German-occupied territory. Although they were officially the enemy, Edith made sure they were treated. Then she went a step further. She arranged to have the soldiers smuggled out of German-occupied Belgium and into the Netherlands, a neutral country.

By the end of 1914, Edith and her team of nurses were HEALING soldiers and civilians from Britain, France, and Belgium, then shepherding them into the Netherlands. Sometimes they were hidden in the hospital while German troops searched the building in an attempt to take them prisoner.

Edith hid some people at her own house, and gave them her OWN money to help them on their way. As she saw it, helping them escape was an extension of helping them heal. It was all about giving them a FUTURE. She was tireless in her work to help others, saying, "I can't stop while there are lives to be saved."

In spring 1915, Edith became aware of a French officer, Georges Gaston Quien, who was being THREATENED by

the German occupiers. So, using her network, she had him **hidden** at the Château de Bellignies (Bellignies Castle), home of the prince and princess of Croy, who were also helping people ESCAPE.

Unfortunately, Quien WASN'T who he said he was. He was actually a **penniless** local man pretending to be a French officer, while working as a Spy for the Germans.

Edith was arrested and taken to prison. Before her trial she admitted, FREELY and PROUDLY, all that she had done – helping around 200 PEOPLE escape north to

58

the Netherlands, many of them passing through her own home.

The German authorities knew that many of the people she SAVED would return to their home countries, heal up, and come back to fight them. They decided that Edith was guilty of **TREASON** against Germany and should be executed. Countries across the world were shocked by this decision. The USA was not yet involved in the war, but called for her life to be spared. Even the German governor of Belgium suggested that Edith should be pardoned

as she had saved so many lives, including the lives of countless injured German soldiers. But the German military chief would NOT listen: Edith would be shot.

The night before her execution, Edith asked to speak to a priest, Reverend H. Stirling Gahan. She told him she was NOT AFRAID of death: "Tell my loved ones that my SOUL I believe is SAFE. My conscience is clear." She was thankful to God for the time in prison, which had given her a rest from earthly distractions.

The next morning, aged just 49, Edith was given a blindfold and marched out to face the firing squad. Some reports say that she refused the blindfold. Whether Edith could see or not, the eyes of the WORLD were on her.

Edith's body was buried near the prison and MANY of her nurses came to pay tribute to their teacher and moral guide. She had been strict in her leadership, but they could see no finer example of someone acting on what they believed in – HELPING OTHERS – and staying true to that right to the end.

Edith's story lived on through the war. She became instantly famous for her act of COURAGE, leading to many new British soldiers joining up to **DEFEND** the country in her memory. Edith became a symbol of what was worth **FIGHTING** for, and how we can help each other as we go.

Edith had always acted on her belief that the **MOST** important thing was to help EVERYONE, no matter who they were. After the war, Edith's body was taken to England for a funeral service at Westminster Abbey. She was then buried at Norwich Cathedral, near where her family lived in Norfolk. She was back home again – although her TRUE HOME, as she saw it, was by God's side.

"STANDING AS I DO IN VIEW OF GOD AND ETERNITY, I REALIZE THAT PATRIOTISM IS NOT ENOUGH. I MUST HAVE NO HATRED OR BITTERNESS TOWARDS ANYONE."

EDITH CAVELL

THINK

- Edith Cavell did her best to help everyone. How difficult is it to help people who have hurt and upset you, or with whom you disagree?

- Edith risked her life to help others and paid the ultimate price. But living for others doesn't always mean laying down your life. How could you put the needs of others first in your day-to-day life?

READ

But I say to you, Love your enemies and pray for those who persecute you, so that you may be sons of your Father who is in heaven.

Matthew 5:44–45a

PRAY

Father of all people, of those we love and of those with whom we disagree,

We are sorry that we fall out with other people. Thank you for Edith Cavell, and for her constant wish to be more like Jesus: healing others and loving her enemies.

Help us to have no hatred or bitterness towards anyone, and to help those around us, whether they're with us or against us.

    Amen.

CHAPTER 6

JESSE OWENS
(1913-1980)

What does it take to stand up to a dictator? When the **LOUDEST, FIERCEST** person tells lies to the world, how can one person find the courage to single-handedly prove him wrong? How would you behave if the eyes of the world were on you?

This is the story of Jesse Owens, a **DETERMINED** African American athlete known as the world's **GREATEST** sportsman in track and field. But he went beyond that by challenging the lies of the world's most evil leader.

It's also a story about some shoes, a handshake, and not one but **FOUR** gold medals. It's also a story of a non-handshake . . . which sounds odd, but will make sense soon, I promise. In fact, I'll shake on it!

James Cleveland Owens was born in Oakville, Alabama, in 1913. J.C., as he was nicknamed, was the youngest of **TEN** children. He and his family were Christians, and his father, Henry, was one of the leaders at his local Baptist church. They were African Americans in a time and place where segregation (keeping black people and white people **separate**) made life **VERY** difficult for them. J.C.'s grandfather had been enslaved, and although slavery was over, its echoes were **EVERYWHERE**.

When J.C. was nine, he and his family moved to Cleveland, Ohio. His family hoped for a better **FUTURE** there because, although black people **STILL** faced discrimination, Ohio had no segregation laws. When J.C. told his new schoolteacher his name was J.C., she **misheard** and called him "Jesse", and the name **stuck**.

Growing up, Jesse worked to help **SUPPORT** his family. One of his jobs was in a shoe repair shop, and very soon young Jesse realized that all he needed to do was put on a pair of **running** shoes, and he felt like he was **flying**.

Running felt freeing to him – he could run anywhere at any speed, **FAST** or **slow** . . . and Jesse ran **FAST**!

Jesse's junior high school coach spotted his **potential** and supported him to train. By high school, he was matching the **WORLD RECORD** by running the 100-yard dash (91 metres) in 9.4 seconds!

In college, Jesse toured athletics championships, but while the crowds in the stadium **applauded** and

SEGREGATION

After slavery was abolished in 1865, the southern states introduced laws that segregated black people and white people. There were separate schools, churches, swimming pools, and housing areas, and even separate spaces on public transport.

The facilities provided were meant to be "separate but equal", but in reality those for black people were always worse than those for white people.

Segregation made the lives of black people difficult, humiliating, and often frightening.

cheered his **SUCCESSES**, it was a *different* story outside the stadium. While his white teammates were supported through college by scholarships, Jesse, in addition to training, had to WORK to support himself. And when he toured with his white teammates, they stayed in nice hotels and ate at good restaurants, but Jesse wasn't allowed. He had to find places where black people were allowed. Jesse must have felt **ANGRY** to be treated this way, but he FOCUSED on being the best athlete he could be.

In May 1935, Jesse was due to compete in the Big Ten Championships. But five days before the meet he *injured*

his back, so it was not certain whether he could compete. Jesse was DETERMINED, and he persuaded his coach to let him try. He went on to achieve FOUR world records in 45 minutes! (I don't know about you, but I can easily go 45 minutes without achieving any world records.) Jesse showed that he, a black man, could run, leap, and hurdle faster, further, and more nimbly than ANYONE on the PLANET.

But across the world, Adolf Hitler, the German leader, was making speech after speech that said the opposite.

Hitler said that the **PERFECT** human had white skin and blond hair. Black people, Jewish people, Roma people, and those with disabilities were not only imperfect, but less than human.

Jesse had qualified for the Olympics in Berlin but now he had a **dilemma**. Many said that he shouldn't compete because it would show support for Hitler's leadership.

Jesse didn't want to show support for Hitler and his **FALSE** ideas, but he also faced segregation and discrimination at home. As a record-breaking athlete, he knew that there was no better place to **PROVE** to the **WORLD** what a black man could do. He chose to compete.

THE 1936 BERLIN OLYMPIC GAMES

Every four years, the summer Olympic Games visits a different country and the world's greatest sportspeople compete against each other. In 1936 it was Germany's turn – a decision made years before Adolf Hitler rose to power.

There were calls from America and Europe to boycott the Olympics (which means to withdraw as a protest), but the Games went ahead. The first ever televised Olympics gave the world a fake impression of Nazism as peaceful and tolerant, rather than racist and fuelled by hatred.

Just before the Games started, the German owner of the Adidas shoe company approached Jesse and gave him the **FIRST EVER** sponsorship deal for a black athlete. Once a shoe repairer, Jesse was now the global face of the *finest* running shoes in the world!

As soon as Jesse arrived at the Berlin stadium, it was clear that the crowd **LOVED** him. It wasn't just American supporters; local spectators also *cheered* and *chanted*: "Where is Jesse? Where is Jesse?"

However, Jesse knew that: "The battles that **COUNT** aren't the ones for gold medals. The struggles *within yourself* – the invisible, inevitable battles inside all of us – that's where it's at."

As the first events began, Hitler shook hands with any Germans who won their events, but *refused* to congratulate anyone else. Hitler was told by the Olympic Committee that he must shake hands with **EVERY** winner or **no** winner at all, so he left.

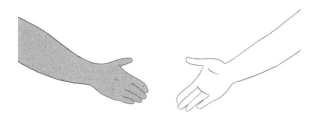

The next day, Jesse WON the gold medal for the 100m sprint. Hitler watched from the stands, quietly FURIOUS that any non-white athlete could be the best.

One of the German athletes – tall, white, blond, just as Hitler wanted – was willing to greet Jesse. Luz Long noticed that, before Jesse competed, he would kneel and pray to God for strength – not just outer strength to win the race, but INNER STRENGTH to face whatever the world threw at him. And the world was throwing A LOT.

Luz was INSPIRED by Jesse's praying, and the two competitors became friends. When they faced each other in the long jump the next day, Jesse won the gold medal and Luz won silver. The African American had BEATEN the blond German! The two athletes walked arm in arm around the stadium, which angered Hitler even more.

Jesse went on to win the gold medal in the 200m sprint and the relay. He won FOUR gold medals in total – as well as breaking WORLD RECORDS!

Hitler's idea of what made a "perfect human" was shown to be ridiculous. No one knew at this time that he would soon drag the world into the DEADLY chaos of the Second World War (you can read more about this in the next chapter).

Jesse returned home, but there was no fame and fortune waiting for him. While the white members of the Olympic team were invited to meet the PRESIDENT, Jesse and the other black athletes were not. When he attended Olympic victory parties, he was forced to use the back door and he STILL wasn't allowed to stay at the same hotels as his white teammates.

Despite the discrimination he continued to face in his home country, Jesse had shown the WORLD what a black man could ACHIEVE. Ideas about non-white people being inferior – whether from Hitler or as suggested by segregation laws – had been proven wrong.

He also had an impact on his fellow competitors. The Owens and Long families kept in touch, and it was said that seeing Jesse pray before his races had helped Luz FIND FAITH in God, too.

Jesse's firm faith, determination, and dignity were INSPIRATIONAL to many people, and he spent his life touring and speaking to youth groups, sports groups, and faith groups. He encouraged people to BELIEVE and TRUST in God's plan and to do the right thing, improving the world one day at a time, one step at a time – running that race of life, and staying focused on the track ahead.

"ONLY BY GOD'S GRACE HAVE I MADE IT TO SEE TODAY, AND ONLY BY GOD'S GRACE WILL I EVER SEE TOMORROW."

JESSE OWENS

THINK

- Jesse worked hard to win races! Is there something you would like to get better at? How could you improve?
- Jesse prayed before his races and relied on God's strength, not his own. Learn the Bible verse below, and the next time you need courage, try repeating it to yourself.

READ

I can do all things through him who strengthens me.

Philippians 4:13

PRAY

God of justice,

Thank you for Jesse Owens – for his faith, determination, and courage to prove that other people's prejudices were wrong. I pray for those who are not treated fairly, for those who are judged because of how they look, and for those who are not given a fair chance. Help me to keep my eyes fixed on you, God, and help me to run my own race through life.

Amen.

CHAPTER 7
CORRIE TEN BOOM
(1892–1983)

Would **you** go out of your way to help others? What would you risk to do so? And if things went from bad to worse, would you **KEEP** trusting in God through the dark times?

This is the story of Corrie ten Boom, a **SELFLESS** Dutch watchmaker who saved the lives of other people by putting herself in **GREAT** danger.

It's also a story about a bell, a secret Bible, and a list. These were all like cogs in a machine, helping Corrie's life tick along. And cogs are something Corrie knew all about . . .

Cornelia ten Boom – Corrie for short – was born into a family of watchmakers in Haarlem, a town in the Netherlands, in 1892. Aged 30, she became the **FIRST** licensed female watchmaker in the country, while also running a Sunday school for teenage girls, sharing her **FAITH**, and teaching them sewing. All was well – until it wasn't . . .

THE SECOND WORLD WAR BEGINS

In January 1933, Adolf Hitler, the leader of the Nazi party, rose to power in Germany, becoming chancellor. He made fierce speeches attacking minority groups, especially Jewish people.

In September 1939, Germany invaded Poland. Two days later, Britain and France declared war on Germany. Europe was at war again.

In May 1940, Germany invaded the Netherlands. Jewish people across Europe feared for their lives, as Hitler's Nazi party tried to arrest, imprison, or wipe them out completely.

Households all around Europe were forced to decide whether to help those in need . . .

When the Nazi party took **CONTROL** of the Netherlands in 1940, Corrie, her father (Casper), and her sister (Betsie), began **hiding** their Jewish friends, and soon Jewish strangers, too. "In this household," Corrie said, "God's people are always WELCOME."

Corrie and her family **sheltered** them for a short while until they could be moved on safely to **another** hiding place, and eventually out of the country. The police headquarters was nearby, so it was **VERY** risky. If they were caught, they would be arrested and perhaps killed.

Soon they ran out of room, and so "room" was exactly what was needed! A new one. Slowly, without suspicion, visitors came to the house to design and provide materials for a secret room. Casper used his precise watchmaking skills to construct a false wall in Corrie's bedroom. Behind it was a room big enough for six people. It was called "The Hiding Place".

Most of the time, their Jewish guests lived relatively **normal** lives with the ten Boom family. They ate with them and slept in beds, but they could **NEVER** risk leaving the house. The police often checked houses without notice, so it was **VITAL** that the hideaways could reach the secret room as quickly as possible.

The family set up a bell system. From anywhere in the house, the bell button could be pushed to act as an **ALARM**. How **quickly** could their guests reach the hiding place? They could never quite get there in under a minute, much as they tried. About 70 seconds was as close as they could manage.

Many times, the police arrived and the hideaways **RACED** upstairs. If they were eating, they took their cutlery and crockery, so it looked like the ten Booms were the only ones dining. If they were sleeping, they **flipped** their mattresses so the police wouldn't feel the warmth of where they had been lying. Around **800** Jewish people were **SAVED** by the ten Boom family.

And then one day there was a loud **THUMPING** knock at the door. The buzzer **BUZZED** and six secret guests ran to the hiding place. A bigger **crash** followed as the front door was broken in by Nazi police. They began

SEARCHING the house, tipped off by a local Dutchman who knew that Corrie's family was HELPING Jewish people. The police quickly found paperwork evidence, and Casper, Corrie, and Betsie were ARRESTED.

While sitting in jail, awaiting trial, Corrie kept wondering if the six guests had been discovered. A coded message reached her: "ALL the watches in your cabinet are SAFE." She knew what this meant: their hiding place had worked. The Jewish refugees had been moved to a new safehouse.

Sisters Corrie and Betsie, both in their 50s by this time, were eventually sent to a concentration camp called Ravensbrück.

Before entering the camp, Corrie and Betsie were FORCED into a line. They had to change into prison camp uniforms, which caused a problem.

Corrie had smuggled in her Bible under her dress, as well as some medicine for Betsie, who was unwell. While changing, Corrie noticed a bench, so she quickly hid the Bible and medicine underneath. Then she put the prison dress on and hid the items underneath it.

Then a new problem appeared: EVERYONE was being searched. Corrie gulped nervously as the guard

CONCENTRATION CAMPS

Concentration camps were set up by the German authorities from 1933. They were a form of prison – not for criminals who had received a fair trial, but for groups of people the Nazis wanted to control.

The camps kept large numbers of people in one place, where they were either put to work or, in many cases, held until they could be killed.

These were very dangerous places, with little food and terrible conditions.

Ravensbrück was a large women's work camp in Germany. And you weren't allowed to take any possessions in.

checked each woman in front of her – but then something **strange** happened. The woman in front was **searched** several times, delaying the line. So Corrie was told to hurry on in. So, when they arrived in Barracks 28, where they were to live with **HUNDREDS** of other women, Corrie's **smuggled** Bible came with them.

At first Corrie felt **miserable**, but Betsie reminded her that they still had each other, God in their lives, and an **AMAZING** group of women around them.

Conditions were **TERRIBLE**, living with bugs and lice, but Corrie soon started THANKING God for those because it meant the guards wanted to go nowhere near the place. Their accommodation remained unchecked, so the Bible was never found. Corrie and Betsie helped **MANY** women come to know Jesus, and Barracks 28 gradually became a place for secret worship. The guards **NEVER** knew that Corrie and Betsie were leading Bible reading, prayer, and praise sessions there.

Betsie shared with Corrie a VISION she had for what they might do after their release: they would set up a HOME to help other concentration camp survivors. But Betsie wasn't well, and in December 1944 she died of ill health at the age of 59.

Twelve days later, Corrie was released . . . by accident, as it turned out. Her name had mistakenly been put on a list of prisoners to be freed. A few days later, all the women Corrie's age were executed at the camp.

Corrie suddenly found herself FREE, on her own, and – INSPIRED by Betsie's vision – filled with new purpose in the outside world.

Despite everything she had suffered at the concentration camp and the risk of being rearrested, Corrie hid MORE people in her new home during the last year of the war. She believed that: "The measure of a life, after all, is not its duration, but its donation."

Then in peacetime she set up a home for camp survivors. AMAZINGLY, she also welcomed Dutch collaborators (people who had helped the Nazis), just like the man whose tip-off had sent the police to her house many years earlier.

83

Corrie helped EVERYONE, whether they were on her side or not.

One day in 1947, Corrie was preaching at a church in Germany. MANY people wanted to hear her story, and MANY wanted to greet her afterwards. But when one man approached her, she froze. She instantly recognized him as a prison guard, one who had been especially cruel to Betsie. The former guard gave Corrie a beaming smile and said, "How GRATEFUL I am for your message . . . To think that, as you say, God has washed my sins away!" He thrust out his hand for Corrie to shake.

Corrie struggled to forgive him and to take his hand. She prayed for help to do so, and as she put her hand in his, the most INCREDIBLE thing happened. She felt a HEALING WARMTH flow through her and into her heart sprang a love that nearly overwhelmed her.

By the time Corrie died, aged 91, she had toured the world, preaching about Jesus' message of FORGIVENESS and LOVE. She had also written many books and had her story made into a film: *The Hiding Place*. One thing Corrie NEVER kept hidden was her faith – worn proudly for the benefit of all around her, WHOEVER they might be.

"IF GOD SENDS US ON STONY PATHS, HE PROVIDES STRONG SHOES."

CORRIE TEN BOOM

THINK

- Corrie and her family risked their lives to help people they didn't know. In what ways could you care for people from other countries and cultures?
- Corrie forgave the people who had hurt her, even the cruel prison guard. How hard is it to forgive those who have been mean to you? Is there anyone you need to ask God to help you forgive?

READ

Let all bitterness and wrath and anger . . . be put away from you, along with all malice. Be kind to one another, tender-hearted, forgiving one another, as God in Christ forgave you.

Ephesians 4:31–32

PRAY

Merciful God,

Thank you for sending your son, Jesus, so that we can be forgiven when we are truly sorry. Thank you for Corrie ten Boom and her family – for the great acts of service they gave, and for Corrie's example of forgiveness. We pray that your loving forgiveness will fill our hearts when we need to forgive others.

Amen.

CHAPTER 8
MARTIN LUTHER KING, JR.
(1929-1968)

So far we've met some incredible HEROES who have done amazing things. Yet the world today is FAR from perfect. So how do we keep looking forward to a brighter future? What vision should we have to work towards? How can we stand up against injustice?

This is the story of Martin Luther King, Jr., an INSPIRATIONAL black church minister and civil rights activist who never settled for the world as it was. Instead, he campaigned for what was right, even risking his life to do so.

It's also a story about a ball, a TV, and a microphone. Thanks to technology, Martin's message went FURTHER and FASTER than anyone else's we've met so far. Tech can be a marvellous thing!

Michael King, Jr. was born in 1929. HOLD ON! Who's that? Yes, this is another of our heroes who changed his name. Michael King, Jr. became Martin Luther King, Jr. when he was 28 years old, but we'll call him Martin from the start.

Martin grew up in Atlanta, Georgia, a segregated state in the USA. He saw how **UNFAIR** segregation was when he was just six years old.

Martin and a white boy from across the street *enjoyed* throwing a ball for fun, but one day when Martin went out to play, his friend's parents said there would be **NO** more playtime, **EVER**. They banned any contact between the young friends, simply because their son had white skin and Martin had black skin.

Martin was *confused*, and this confusion turned to **ANGER** when his parents explained the history of slavery. His father, Martin Luther King, Sr., was an activist and a church minister who urged his son to LOVE everyone and to respond PEACEFULLY, but he also taught him **NEVER** to accept this system of racism.

As Martin grew up, he followed in his father's *footsteps*. He studied hard to gain a **GREAT** education and was soon a minister, leading a church of his own. He was determined to **FIGHT** the injustices he saw and to HELP those who were suffering in front of him.

In 1955, Martin was a LEADER in what became known as the Montgomery Bus Boycott. This was sparked by two black women, Claudette Colvin and Rosa Parks, on two different bus rides, who REFUSED to give up their seats to white people. Martin helped to lead a campaign to boycott the city's buses: for over a YEAR, many black people refused to travel by bus.

Those who were against Martin tried to scare him into backing down. They even bombed his house. Martin's first response, before even checking his family was OK (they were), was to urge his friends and followers NOT to fight back. The bus company lost a fortune in fares and, in 1956, segregation on buses was BANNED.

By this time, Martin was the best-known civil rights activist in the country. He firmly believed that God had created ALL PEOPLE EQUAL and that Christians were called to make the world a fairer place, but ONLY by using peaceful methods. He was inspired by Mahatma Gandhi, an Indian Hindu activist, who thought that the best response to VIOLENCE was nonviolence. Of course, as a Christian, Martin's greatest inspiration was Jesus, and he followed Jesus' example of LOVING his enemies.

Martin's enemies tried all sorts of things to stop his speeches and campaigns. They spied on him, listened in

THE CIVIL RIGHTS MOVEMENT

In 1954, the civil rights movement in America began. Its aim was to end discrimination against black people and to abolish segregation so that they had the same access as white people to services such as schools and hospitals, plus the same job opportunities, and equal protection under the law.

Although black people had the right to vote, it was extremely hard for them to do so in many southern states. The states imposed voting taxes, which black people could not afford, and literacy tests, which many failed because they had been denied a good education. They also faced violence and intimidation if they tried to vote. The civil rights movement campaigned for these barriers to voting to be made illegal.

to his phone calls, and had him arrested ... **29 TIMES**! Sometimes it was for driving too **FAST**, other times he was arrested for **peaceful** "sit-in" protests, where he and others sat in restaurants that discriminated against black people. Even from jail, Martin's words needed to be heard, so on one occasion he wrote a speech on prison **toilet paper**, then had it **smuggled** out, typed up, and distributed.

In 1963, Martin led a campaign in Birmingham, Alabama, that involved **BREAKING** segregation laws by marching or staging "sit-ins" in white-only spaces. The police didn't know how to respond, so they *panicked* and used police dogs and water cannons, sometimes even on children.

At the time, the popularity of TV news was *growing*, and when news cameras started filming these scenes, many white people across the country **FINALLY** saw why the civil rights movement was **DESPERATELY NEEDED**. Many joined the campaign. Soon, some of the segregation laws **CHANGED**, and black people were able to eat and shop in some of the same places as white people.

With America's eyes on them, Martin and his friends went bigger and bolder. A **HUGE** march was planned for Washington D.C., the nation's capital. The march would end with speeches at the Lincoln Memorial, a **MASSIVE** monument dedicated to President Abraham Lincoln, which symbolized determined leadership, **FREEDOM**, and union.

None of the other leaders wanted to speak after Martin, who was known as one of the world's **GREATEST** public speakers. Practice makes perfect . . . in one year, he had given 350 **SPEECHES** in 365 **DAYS**! They decided Martin had to be the last to speak to the crowd.

Standing in front of the microphone at the end of a long day, Martin saw some of the crowd start to leave to get the train home. He needed to give the **SPEECH** of his **LIFE**.

THE MARCH ON WASHINGTON

A quarter of a million people attended the march on Washington – it was the largest protest the city had ever seen. The protesters demanded an end to segregation and showed their support for newly proposed civil rights laws.

The leaders of six big civil rights groups headed up the march and spoke to the crowd. Famous singers and actors such as Sidney Poitier, Charlton Heston, Bob Dylan, Mahalia Jackson, and Marlon Brando all turned up to support it.

President John F. Kennedy did not attend the march, but he greeted the leaders afterwards at the White House.

He read his prepared speech, talking about the history of slavery and segregation, and what black people were owed by the country that had promised **EVERYONE** "life, LIBERTY and the pursuit of happiness".

The singer Mahalia Jackson then yelled over to him: "Tell them about the *dream*, Martin!" So he did:

> I have a dream that my four little children will one day live in a nation where they will not be judged by the color of their skin but by the content of their character.

He spoke freely and passionately about his dream for the nation's future: one of HOPE and UNITY. It became known as one of the greatest speeches EVER given.

A year later – in the hundredth year since the end of slavery – the government passed the Civil Rights Act, making racial segregation and discrimination ILLEGAL. Martin won the Nobel Peace Prize the same year. But he had more to fight for, as black people STILL didn't have the same voting rights as white people.

So, in 1965, Martin and others marched from Selma to Montgomery, two cities in Alabama. They PRAYED to God as they walked, looking forward to a future of joy and unity. But the police blocked their path. In some cases they were VIOLENT against the peaceful protesters. Many people were injured, and some died. Again, TV news cameras made sure that the protest of thousands was seen by MILLIONS.

The protest worked, leading to the Voting Rights Act of 1965. But the violence continued. Three years later, after speaking in support of equal pay for black workers, Martin was SHOT and killed. He had avoided so many attacks on his life, but he couldn't escape this one.

Each year, the USA celebrates Martin Luther King, Jr. Day, to remember the GREAT work he did in bringing freedom, equality, and unity to others. He BRAVELY battled injustice and fought for equality, but only ever with words and PEACEFUL actions. The child who hadn't been allowed to play with his friend grew up to make sure MILLIONS of others could play with theirs.

"DARKNESS CANNOT DRIVE OUT DARKNESS; ONLY LIGHT CAN DO THAT. HATE CANNOT DRIVE OUT HATE; ONLY LOVE CAN DO THAT."

MARTIN LUTHER KING, JR.

THINK

- Martin had a dream of a better world. What would a perfect world look like for you? What do you think God's vision of a perfect world might be?

- Martin knew that black people were being treated unequally and did something about it. Who do you see being treated unfairly? What could you do about it?

READ

There is neither Jew nor Greek, there is neither slave nor free, there is no male and female, for you are all one in Christ Jesus.

Galatians 3:28

PRAY

Creator God, who made all people in your image,

We are sorry when we don't treat others equally and for the times when we go along with unfairness. Thank you for Martin Luther King, Jr., and for all who have stood up against discrimination, in peace, love, and hope. Help us to treat others with dignity and respect. May we all play and live together well.

Amen.

FANTASTICALLY FAITHFUL FINAL THOUGHTS

WOW! What amazing lives we've learned about and what inspirational people we've met!

What does all that mean for us, then?

Sometimes we can look at brilliantly inspiring HEROES and think: "GREAT . . . but what can I do? I'm just . . . me!"

Well, many of our heroes thought just the same thing. Yet each of them had such great FAITH in God, and such a good understanding of what was best for humanity, that they heroically made a difference to this world of ours.

Maybe they weren't thinking about big, giant, HUGE humanity at all. Maybe they were just looking to help the people in front of them.

Helping everyone in the world may seem just a little bit too daunting! But when we think about what these eight people had in common, perhaps it's that they all tried to care for those in front of their very noses, in the best way they could.

They tried to FIX the problem in front of them, to HEAL the wound in front of them, to LOVE the people in front of them.

Perhaps, then, if we help those around us – whoever they are – equally, we'll all be doing our bit to help the world, one act of kindness at a time.

We don't have to get it right the first time. It can be a challenge. Each of our HEROES had their own problems, too. Some didn't get along with their families or friends. Some were strict or stubborn. Some didn't ALWAYS make the right choices. They didn't get EVERYTHING right, ALL the time. But they kept focused on God, and what he wanted, and I think our lives are better for having shared the planet with these FANTASTICALLY FAITHFUL HEROES.

Each Christmas at the church I go to, the minister says a special blessing to remind us of the best qualities of the first people (and angels!) who met Jesus. You may have heard it yourself:

> May the joy of the angels,
> the eagerness of the shepherds,
> the perseverance of the wise men,
> the obedience of Joseph and Mary,
> and the peace of the Christ child
> be yours this Christmas . . .

Perhaps we can create a new **blessing** to end this book – to remind us of eight people who weren't the first to meet Jesus, but I'm sure met him at some point, and were inspired to make a difference. Not only that, they still **INSPIRE** others to make a difference today!

So here's my blessing for **you** . . .

May the generosity of Edward Jenner,
the prayerful courage of Harriet Tubman,
the dedication of Pandita Ramabai,
the enthusiastic faith of John Harper,
the all-embracing love of Edith Cavell,
the inner strength of Jesse Owens,
the forgiveness of Corrie ten Boom,
the sense of justice of Martin Luther King, Jr.,
and the uniqueness of you,
be yours this day and throughout your lifetime,
and the blessing of God almighty,
the Father, the Son, and the Holy Spirit,
be among you and remain with you always.
Amen.

I hope you've enjoyed learning about these frankly **BRILLIANT** individuals. I hope now and then as you go through life, you'll **think** about some of their lives, or even just little moments that made a **BIG** difference: Corrie ten Boom testing how quickly her house guests could **hide** in her bedroom; John Harper swimming up to that survivor to **TELL** him about God; Harriet Tubman making her chickens **squawk** to make a quick getaway (I don't know if I'd have been brave enough to do that)!

Because sometimes it's the little decisions, just as much as the **BIG** ones, that make the difference, such as Edith Cavell choosing to **HELP** an enemy soldier or Martin Luther King, Jr. telling a quarter of a million people about his **dream**!

I wonder what your dream is. Your **VISION** for the world. Maybe you could write it down somewhere and see – each day, bit by bit, moment by moment – if you can make it come **TRUE**.

Also available in this series

ACKNOWLEDGEMENTS

p. 16: Edward Jenner quotation taken from *The Life of Edward Jenner: With Illustrations and Selections from His Correspondence* by John Baron (1838), p. 295.

p. 20: Harriet Tubman quotation taken from *Harriet Tubman: A biography* by James A. McGowan and William C. Kashatus (Bloomsbury Publishing USA, 2011), p. 51.

p. 22–23 : Harriet Tubman quotation taken from https://torchlighters.org/harriet-tubman-the-moses-of-her-people/ (accessed January 2025)

p. 23: Harriet Tubman quotation taken from https://canonjjohn.com/2020/08/08/heroes-of-the-faith-harriet-tubman/ (accessed January 2025)

p. 26: Harriet Tubman quotation taken from *Harriet Tubman: The life and life* stories by Jean Humez (University of Wisconsin Press, 2003), p. 228.

p. 28: Harriet Tubman quotation taken from https://archive.org/details/harriettubmanlif0000hume/mode/2up?q=%22I+always+told+him%22 (accessed January 2025)

p. 34: Pandita Ramabai quotation taken from *Pandita Ramabai: Life and landmark writings* by Meera Kosambi (Routledge India, 2018).

p.36: Pandita Ramabai quotation taken from https://christianhistoryinstitute.org/magazine/article/ch-144-twenty-centuries-of-christian-quotes (accessed January 2025)

p. 49: Titanic survivor quotation taken from https://www.moodymedia.org/articles/sharing-gift-christmas-one-minute-you-die/ (accessed January 2025)

p. 51: John Harper quotation taken from https://www.scotsman.com/news/opinion/columnists/titanic-sinking-how-scots-preacher-john-harper-came-to-be-hailed-the-bravest-man-on-that-boat-susan-morrison-4588667 (accessed January 2025)

p. 57, 60: Edith Cavell quotations taken from https://edithcavell.org.uk/edith-cavell-in-her-own-words/ (accessed January 2025)

p. 62: Edith Cavell quotation taken from https://edithcavell.org.uk/edith-cavells-life/account-by-reverend-h-stirling-gahan-on-the-execution-of-edith-cavell/ (accessed January 2025)

p. 70: Jesse Owens quotation taken from http://jesseowensmemorialpark.com/wordpress1/links-facts/ (accessed January 2025)

p. 74: Jesse Owens quotation taken from https://everydaypower.com/jesse-owens-quotes/ (accessed January 2025)

p. 83: Corrie ten Boom quotation taken from https://www.biography.com/activists/corrie-ten-boom (accessed January 2025)

p. 84: Copyright © *The Hiding Place* by Corrie ten Boom (Hodder & Stoughton, 1972), p. 241.

p. 85: Corrie Ten Boom quotation taken from *The Lion Christian Quotation Collection* compiled by Hannah Ward and Jennifer Wild (Lion Publishing, 1997), p. 234.

p. 94: *Strength to Love* by Martin Luther King, Jr. copyright © reprinted by arrangements of The Heirs of the Estate of Martin Luther King, Jr., c/o Writers House as agent for the proprietor New York, N.Y. Copyright © 1963 by Dr. Martin Luther King, Jr. Renewed © 1991 by Coretta Scott King.

p. 97: "I Have a Dream" speech by Martin Luther King, Jr. is reprinted by arrangements of The Heirs of the Estate of Martin Luther King, Jr., c/o Writers House as agent for the proprietor New York, N.Y. Copyright © 1963 by Dr. Martin Luther King, Jr. Renewed © 1991 by Coretta Scott King.